Grace

Grace

MICHAEL LEWIS
MACLENNAN

Grace
first published 1998 by
Scirocco Drama
An imprint of J. Gordon Shillingford Publishing Inc.

Reprinted March 2001

Scirocco Drama Editor: Dave Carley
Cover design by Terry Gallagher/Doowah Design Inc.
Cover illustration is a detail from Panel 5 of "Paintings for Dimly Lit Rooms" Series
by Wanda Koop
Author Photo by Kathryn Gaitens
Printed and bound in Canada

We acknowledge the financial support of The Canada Council for the Arts and the Manitoba Arts Council for our publishing program.

Canadian Cataloguing in Publication Data

MacLennan, Michael Lewis, 1968–
Grace
A play.
ISBN 1-896239-34-X
I. Title.
PS8575.L46G73 1998 C812'.54 C98-900114-8
PR9199.3.M33412G73 1998

Grace is dedicated to Michael Hoppe,
who taught me the meaning of the word.

Acknowledgements

So many people have lent support. I particularly thank Peter Hinton, who has inhabited this play with love and helped me to make it the best I could. Glynis Leyshon and Bob White helped make *Grace* a reality. Gina Wilkinson was a tireless and inspired collaborator. I acknowledge the fine actors who performed in the early productions and also those who workshopped this play (especially Bill Dow, Michael Healey, Wendy Noel, Maralyn Ryan and Meredith Bain Woodward). I also thank Sam Buggeln, Dave Carley, Shelley Darjes, Mary Desprez, Michael Dobbin, Mark Dusseault, Marina Endicott, Andrew Gillies, Amiel Gladstone, Cora Golden, Chapelle Jaffe, Jennifer Lord, David Owen Lucas, David Mackay, Lori MacLennan, Kim McCaw, Andrew Mellen, Bob Milne, Rob Moffatt, Brian Pace, Michelle Porter, Brigitte Potter-Mäl, Dianne Searle, Rick Searle, Sandhano Schultze, Edel Strassmann, Iris Turcott, Randy White, Peter Wilds; Alberta Theatre Projects, Banff Playwrights Colony, Belfry Theatre, Playwrights Theatre Centre and Theatre B.C.

Playwright's Notes

Grace began in transit. I lived and travelled in cities alone and, like the characters in the play, I was in trouble.

To me, *Grace* has grown to be about the tender act of watching, about society's ability to care for itself, about the nature of home and what living in a city does to us, about the temper of our superficial judgments—and about that remarkable web to which we are largely oblivious.

The play makes references to angels. But instead of the benevolent guardian spirits of our popular mythology, they are a different kind of angel: strangers with startling intelligence and often unwelcome messages—angels who are ignored, mocked, fled from. As Rainer Maria Rilke wrote, "Every angel is terrifying."

Paula asks, "Don't strange things ever happen to you?" I think our answer is Yes only when we are on the edge of things, only when we are desperate or foolish enough to be ensnared by fate and open to the discreet mercy of strangers. There are fleeting times in our lives—we've all been on the receiving and giving ends—in which something strange *does* happen. Words miraculously tumble from us, touching another, or some stranger wrestles our soul, transforming us. The experience of those fleeting moments of meaningful contact inspired me to write *Grace*.

Cast

Hugh, 50:	Puffy; expensive suit.
Jared, 22:	Beautiful, lean.
Lonnie, 39:	Poised, elegant, clean.
Thomas, 30:	Blunt, mentally retarded.
Ruth, 60s:	Ornery, frayed. Nothing romantic.
Paula, 23:	Big, insecure. Severe eczema on her hands.

Setting

City. Public spaces. One day.

Spaces should be described by only key set pieces, lights and sound. The key is verisimilitude: everything used—from bus seats to flowers to money—must be utterly real to us. Costuming should avoid totemic stereotypes and instead serve the idiosyncratic expression of the actors.

The City

A few subtle references set the play in Vancouver, B.C. However, if desired, the play may be adapted to fit the location where the play is produced. A guide at the end of the play lists the lines where minor alterations may be made.

Line Ends

...	Line fades.
—	Line interrupted by following line.
/	Line interrupted by following line at slash insertion point.

Production History

Grace was first produced March, 1997 by the Belfry Theatre, Victoria, with the following cast and crew:

Hugh	John Krich
Jared	Todd Witham
Lonnie	Jan Wood
Thomas	Paul Terry
Ruth	Susan Hogan
Paula	Julia Mackey

Directed by Gina Wilkinson
Set and Costume design by David Owen Lucas
Lighting Design by Adam Wilkinson
Sound Design by Gina Wilkinson
Stage Manager: Kate Wallace

The play was developed through the Belfry Theatre, Playwrights Theatre Centre and the Playwrights Colony at the Banff Centre for the Arts.

Subsequently revised, *Grace* received its premiere by Alberta Theatre Projects at the Martha Cohen Theatre, Calgary on February 6, 1998, with the following cast and crew:

Hugh	Andrew Gillies
Jared	Christian Goutsis
Lonnie	Tracey Ferencz
Thomas	Tom Rooney
Ruth	Valerie Ann Pearson
Paula	Julia Mackey

Directed by Peter Hinton
Assisted by Edel Strassmann
Set Design by Scott Reid
Costume Design by Judith Bowden
Lighting Design by Brian Pincott
Sound Design by John Bent Jr.
Stage Manager: Neil Scott
Assistant Stage Manager: Karen Thirlwall

Michael Lewis MacLennan

Born in Vancouver, Michael Lewis MacLennan's first play *Beat the Sunset* won the Sidney Risk Award for outstanding emerging playwright and the *Theatrum* National Playwriting Award. His next major play, *Grace,* won the Theatre BC National Playwriting Competition and has been performed in England and across Canada. His play *The Shooting Stage* won the Herman Voaden National Playwriting Competition. Other plays include *Leaning Over Railings* and *The Fabulous Life*. His new play *Last Romantics* is the first ever commission from the Shaw Festival. Now living in Toronto, Michael also writes for film and television.

suspension

(Transit, dawn. HUGH, a businessman in an expensive suit, tail end of a drinking jag, sits next to JARED, rough-looking in a leather jacket, army boots, tight jeans and unruly, spiked hair. Today's newspaper in his lap, JARED looks out the window.)

HUGH: Nice sunrise. Me, I never ride these things. I drive or get driven.

Crashed my car last night. Was in no shape to call the cops, you know what I mean. Probably still there, wrapped around the tree. Boxes from the office in the back seat: books, photos and stuff. No good to anybody but that won't stop some shithead from stealing it.

So. You got tattoos? They're permanent, you know. I got a tattoo on my arm, people at work never knew. *(Starts to show it.)* See, I was in the navy, your age, got out of the piss-hole town I grew up in, and I uh… Welllll, not much of a story. Where you got tattoos?

(Of newspaper.) Looking for work? Reading the horoscopes. Personals? You have a listing, hey? What would it say: cute young punk, what: twenty-four, twenty-three? Seeks…seeks what. Seeks same? Or different. How d'you get your hair like that.

(JARED turns to regard HUGH, almost frightening him.)

Your hair…

JARED: Egg.

HUGH: Oh. Egg. Beauty secrets, huh?*(Pause.)* So you hear the story about the angel of the bridge? She's famous now, heard of her? Well two weeks ago this woman's driving along a bridge and out of the corner of her eye she catches sight of a man up in the wires, getting ready to jump. So she slams on the brakes, practically causes a smash-up, and runs back to where she saw him. He was still there so she just reaches up her hand and touches his, his leg and…she talks to him. There's this huge traffic jam and it's pissing rain but she stands there for three hours, touching his foot. And there's police and helicopters and cameras everywhere, but really it's just this guy and this woman, stranger, who's talking to him and she won't let anybody else come near and finally, I don't know what she said…but he finally came down. Police snatch him up and she drives off. Gets home, the news are swarming her. It was great, she didn't know what she was getting into. Now everybody wants to talk to her. They're going to give her a radio show where she helps screwed-up people on the air. That way everybody else can hear.

JARED: Which bridge.

HUGH: What?

JARED: Which bridge was—

HUGH: I don't know which bridge, it was on television.

JARED: Hm.

HUGH: I was working late with the TV on. Doesn't seem to bother me. You uh… You know, you got this line—

(Reaches. JARED flinches.)

Woah! It's just, you got pen on your face! Christ.

JARED: Where.

HUGH: Right…there.

(JARED wipes his face.)

Probably had it on all night. So. What were you out all night for, hey? *(Mustering levity.)* Hey you bad boy? You get lucky? Hey?

I been pretty lucky—with work I mean. I got a track record—hell, I was on the news so many times my kid he stopped videotaping me. Shoulda seen me work a room, keeping my right hand dry and warm for shaking. Yeah, I been to all the airports, kept suits in Toronto and Chicago. I used to be your size too. You, what: twenty-two? Twenty-one? You'd have no problem getting a job: you put the boss there… Hey, you listening?

JARED: Yeah.

HUGH: Good. So you put him there and us here, and you know who he'd pick? You. Why? You're a strapping young man. And everybody wants to hire strapping young men.

(Of crash.) You shoulda seen my car. *(Sad laugh.)* What am I gonna do…

I'm gonna be straight with you. I'm wondering…I was wondering, what do you…what do you say we… *(Beat.)* What do you suppose she said to him, hey?

JARED: Don't know.

HUGH: You'd've done it, hey? Rescue him?

JARED: I'd keep going.

HUGH: Oh come on, no you wouldn't, think about it.

JARED: I'd be on a bus, I couldn't stop.

HUGH: You'd tell the driver, you'd stop if you could.

JARED: You can't stop somebody from dying.

HUGH: Sure you can: that woman, she stopped him.

JARED: Then he was never gonna jump.

HUGH: What, you saying…you saying it was some kind of…*publicity* stunt?!

JARED: No, if you're really going to kill yourself then nobody can stop you.

HUGH: So if you saw him you'd—what, *nothing*?

JARED: It's a big city, all right? Things like that're always happening. You can't start getting involved.

HUGH: Come on, you're *walking by*...

JARED: Okay, if I was *walking* and was on the same side of the bridge, I'd stop. I mean, he'd be right above me. But I wouldn't know what to say and I'd never think to touch his leg...

HUGH: ...Sure you would....

JARED: ...I wouldn't. So then he'd jump and I'd blame myself.

HUGH: He wouldn't jump, not after seeing your face looking up at him...

JARED: It doesn't happen like that.—

HUGH: Sure it—

JARED: —"Looking up on a bridge", you think that's all it takes?

HUGH: *(Beat.)* I don't know.

JARED: Well don't drag me into this.

HUGH: What do you mean, hey, I'm not—I'm not "dragging" you anywhere, kid. Huh? I'm just sitting next to you. We're just talking.

Where's your stop? Got one of these new condos up here. Nice place: seventeenth floor, good neighbours. Had it two years now, pretty much home. I could buy you breakfast. You look like you need a good, you know...meal. Or we could do something else and I could just, you know, give you money for your own breakfast. I'm not tired. You got things you can do, things people will pay for. What do you—

JARED: How much.

HUGH: (*Startled.*) You serious?

JARED: What would you pay?

HUGH: Well how much do you usually charge…

JARED: Don't ask me, you're the one who should know.

HUGH: Hey, I want you to know that I *never do this*. This is special.

(Each man looks at the other, assessing.)

JARED: Right.

HUGH: What would you say.

JARED: What's it worth to you?

HUGH: What are *you* worth?

(JARED turns away; second thoughts.)

What's your name. So I can think of you, after.

JARED: (*Looking out.*) Philip.

(JARED grabs his jacket and inhales deeply. HUGH watches him.)

HUGH: Philip. My stop'll be coming up. What do you say, should I ring the bell? Hey—you, you…

(JARED begins to cry softly.)

What're you doing? What, what did I…? Don't bail on me now, kid. Philip, this is my stop here, okay? Come off the bus, I'll fix you up. Hot bath, no strings, just a leg up sort of thing.

(His head averted, JARED pushes him away, his outstretched arm holding the newspaper.)

It's just my hand, take it.

(JARED shoves the newspaper at him.)

box

(Bench in a courtyard/square. LONNIE sits wearing sunglasses, looking up at the office building across the street, only her purse beside her. She waits, calming herself. She gingerly presses one cheekbone.

THOMAS arrives. From his jacket's breast pocket he brings out a small cardboard box, a pet caddy used to carry a small bird or rodent home from the pet store. He curls tenderly around the box, peering into its one small hole. He begins to flick the box with a finger.

LONNIE watches.)

LONNIE: What are you doing?

THOMAS: Nothing.

LONNIE: Is there anything in—

THOMAS: It's a' animal. You want it?

LONNIE: No, thank you.

THOMAS: 'Cause I could get another one. It's cheap. Cheep! *(Laughs. Flicking.)* You could eat it.

LONNIE: Ahh, don't do that.

THOMAS: It's okay. It likes it. I got it from the pet store.

LONNIE: So how long has it been in there?

THOMAS: Just one night, I kept it warm in my jacket. It's alive.

LONNIE: Of course it's alive.

THOMAS: It has to stay alive.

LONNIE: Exactly.

THOMAS: Because I have to take it home and kill it. I have a snake.

LONNIE: In there?! You have a—

THOMAS: At home. I'm his little mom. If I didn't feed him he'd die. He's getting bigger, LOTS bigger. Two hamsters each month. An' if they're dead beforehand he won't eat them. Takes him all day to get it inside. Antonia, she's our house leader? I don't h-heed her. I got my own phone you know. She says I feed him too much but she doesn't know anything.

LONNIE: That's a strange way to spend your money.

THOMAS: Well he's MINE, I can do this!

(THOMAS shakes the box at her.)

LONNIE: Hey! Gentle.

THOMAS: What do you care.

(He shakes the box vigorously.)

LONNIE: You stop that! You are torturing a defenceless animal!

(THOMAS shakes it.)

Don't do that!

(LONNIE grabs the box from him.)

THOMAS: Give it! It's not yours, give it!

LONNIE: Then you treat it properly.

THOMAS: NO! Give it! I like it, I like hurting them.

LONNIE: Is there anything—?

THOMAS: Yes, give it!

LONNIE: *(Holding the box.)* Shh, wait. It's not moving.

THOMAS: *(Quiet.)* You can h-hear it sliding around. Slide him, you can hear.

(She does, hearing some faint response.)

He's not dead. When I open the box, that's when he dies.

(With sudden rage and force THOMAS shouts, attacking her.)

Aaahhhhhh!

LONNIE: *(Her desperate fright triggered, she panics, instantly submissive.)* Please don't… Here—please don't…

THOMAS: *(Grabbing the box back.)* You shouldn't've took my box.

LONNIE: *(Up, breathless.)* I thought you… I thought you were going to—

THOMAS: Weirdness weirdness everywhere weirdness. You know about a snake's skin?

LONNIE: Will you shut up for five minutes!

THOMAS: "Ready in fiiive minutes."

(LONNIE looks at her watch.)

Time for work?

(LONNIE looks up at the building, THOMAS too.)

You work in that building?

LONNIE: *(Delayed reaction, now pushing back.)* Don't *grab* me—why did you GRAB me?

THOMAS: OW. *(Pushing back.)* Don't.

LONNIE: Don't push me around like that. Don't you *ever* attack a woman like that.

THOMAS: I didn't mean to.

LONNIE: Well you learn to control yourself or somebody's going to lock you up. Who do you think you are?

THOMAS: I don't know.

LONNIE: *(Relinquishing.)* I wasn't going to...harm it.

THOMAS: What would you do with it. Rescue it? How do you save a hamster. Take him home, to a cage? Huh? To your homey home?

LONNIE: Look, I'm sorry.

THOMAS: It's okay...

LONNIE: You just...provoked me. I think you should take your mouse—

THOMAS: *Hamster.*

LONNIE: Well take it home and put it out of its misery.

THOMAS: NO. Guess what. Sometimes I say F-OFF to Antonia, I'm *not going home*, and then I don't. So what if I live in a group home, she can't make me. My snake can handle it.

(LONNIE takes her glasses off. Her eyes are heavily made up; one is subtly puffy and bruised. She looks up at the building.)

Are you a mom?

LONNIE: *(Pause.)* No.

THOMAS: My mom's dead. Is yours?

LONNIE: No.

THOMAS: She could be.

LONNIE: Someone would call.

THOMAS: Maybe they forgot. I got a telephone, you know. My mom left when I was four. I was TOO MUCH TROUBLE! Oh I was always getting into trouble.

LONNIE: What's your name.

THOMAS: Thomas. You could phone me if you wanted to.

LONNIE: Tell me something, Thomas. *(She turns to him.)* How do I look to you.

(She stands, anxious under his scrutiny.)

THOMAS: Fine.

LONNIE: Good. Do I look...normal?

THOMAS: No.

(Shaken, LONNIE turns away, puts her sunglasses back on and looks at the building in silence.)

You work in that building?

LONNIE: *(Deciding.)* Not today.

THOMAS: You want to come to my place? We could eat breakfast and I could sh-show you my snake.

LONNIE: *(A slight laugh despite herself.)* Uh, no thanks.

THOMAS: Can't bite you. S-squeezes you instead. Till you can't breathe.

LONNIE: Why would you want a snake?

THOMAS: I'm allowed. I'm allowed to kill these little animals. I like watching it. Breaks down everything: bones, hairs, eyeballs. You know what? I have all the snakeskins on my wall. You know what they look like? Dry little s-skins? Guess what they look like.

LONNIE: What.

THOMAS: Rubbers. *(Childish giggles. LONNIE moves away.)* Do you know a woman named Margaret?

LONNIE: No.

THOMAS: I do. You know the thing about her? She wrote me a letter, and—

LONNIE: Look, I'm sorry, but I really...

THOMAS: You gotta go. I know. Because you know what I am? I'm the opposite of deaf.

(LONNIE turns to regard him a moment, musters a nod, and then walks off.)

(Quiet.) And I can hear you. *(Calling after her.)* Okay! Well, bye! Bye!

(THOMAS stands, his box close to his chest. He then lets himself fall to the ground. He lies in the fetal position, his arm outstretched above him, swerving the box around as if it were a toy airplane.)

grave

(Cemetery. RUTH, her ratty plastic bags scattered around her, and JARED with flowers. Each is at a grave, one gravestone between them. As the scene begins both are looking down at their respective deceased beloved. JARED is absorbed in his grief. RUTH talks to her husband's grave in a half-whispered, crazed conversation. NB: RUTH constantly has a candy in her mouth. They protect her, she believes, from bad forces when she is outdoors. Before she finishes one she unwraps another and with a small ceremony, pops it into her mouth.)

RUTH: So I stopped eating grapefruits. I'm fed up splitting them. I know, hey listen, I know it's easy to save the other half. Don't tell me that, I know, upside down on a saucer in the fridge. Dries out in a day in there. I KNOW, Arthur. Can't cut all those fiddly little wedges just to sit down and scoop 'em out. Too fussy. Don't like it by myself. *(Pause.)* So now we're getting slugs in your garden because I got no peels to stick in the flower beds to trap 'em with. To kill 'em. We sure killed a lot of slugs with all those grapefruits. Bastard. Your garden's all going to seed. *(Kicks at the turf around the grave.)* Well don't blame me, bastard!

(RUTH snaps a look at JARED who has gradually forgotten his grief to become fascinated in the woman beside him.)

Who're you?

JARED: Sorry.

(Pause. RUTH kicks again.)

You'll make holes.

RUTH: It'll grow back. He was a lousy golfer, he made holes. *(Kicking.)* Bastard, why'd you make so many holes. *(Beat. To JARED.)* You're new.

JARED: Two months.

RUTH: Look like you should try some kicking. You're not pulling through.

JARED: No. *(Breaks.)*

RUTH: Hey. *(Gruff.)* Hey, now don't start crying—Hey hey, NOT HERE. Come on.

JARED: Sorry.

RUTH: These things sneak up on you.

JARED: Yeah. It was a shock.

RUTH: Well thank Christ for that. Don't want to see her wasting away for months and months like I did. Kids?

JARED: Pardon?

RUTH: You got kids?

JARED: Do I look like I have kids?

RUTH: Look like you wanna scare people away is what you want.

JARED: Well I don't have kids.

RUTH: Arthur and me, we had a son. Oh my lord Mohammed—she, it wasn't, wasn't in…?

JARED: WHAT.

RUTH: Childbirth!

JARED: Uh, no…you're—

RUTH: Thank the Buddha for that one. Lost my sister that way.

JARED: That doesn't kill many people these days.

RUTH: No, I guess they got new things now.

JARED: Yeah.

RUTH: I had a son.

(They look at their respective graves.)

Find another girl. Don't wait. Grief grinds into you, kid. Never get it out, like sand in a bathing suit. Marks you and nobody likes the look of it. He died, I got a drip in the bathroom faucet. Drove me crazy besides wasting water. Finally so fed up I got underneath and turned the bugger off. No water, no drip. Washed myself in the kitchen for a while and then just couldn't be bothered. Sometimes I'd forget, go into the bathroom and turn it on. No water, just a low moaning from the bottom of the house. Gets inside you, son: sorrow, shuts everything down.

(Silence. She slowly moves toward the gravestone near JARED and looks—gapes—down. Finally:)

(Reads.) Philip.

JARED: Yeah.

RUTH: Your…

JARED: My lover.

RUTH: Was named Philip.

JARED: Yes.

RUTH: Hm. So what kind of word is "lover"; that's someone who loves you, not somebody *you* love.

JARED: I loved him.

RUTH: Course you did, you were *his* lover, right? My husband wouldn't've liked, uh, Philip much.

JARED: Phil probably wouldn't have liked your husband.

RUTH: Good thing there's this guy in between them. *(Gathering bags.)* Well I gotta go feed things.

JARED: So I guess I'll see you then.

RUTH: *(Stops. To the grave.)* SHUSH! I'm leaving now, Arthur! *(To JARED.)* He never shuts up. I try and make it so here's the only place I'll talk back. But sometimes I can't help it. He just…*gets* at me.

JARED: I talk to Phil.

RUTH: Well don't. Gets you into trouble. *(Shuffling off.)* I don't wanna see you again. Go home.

JARED: (*Trying to keep her*.) I got a nice home. With Phil. I'd just moved here, six months ago, came from Manitoba, small town. Had to leave.

RUTH: You're young to leave home.

JARED: But I met Phil right away, first bar I went into. He sort of picked me up. Lifted me up. Saved me. We got this great apartment, top floor. Maxed out my new credit cards decorating it and everything. I had a job then. Two months behind on the rent now. But you should see this place. Some days now I just stay in and clean it, look after it. It's where he died. / Home.

RUTH: *(Sotto mumbling.)* Viciousviciousvicious…. *Move on.*

JARED: You keep coming here…

RUTH: I have to tell him things. All the stories, and I'm falling behind. If he knew how fast things really went, it'd kill him. Hell, I stopped eating grapefruit after the bag ran out, week after he died.

JARED: Don't you think he, well, knows?

RUTH: What're you talkin' about—he knows what I tell him! Oh how in Hell, Hades and Gehenna do I know what he knows. *(At voices.)* SHUSH, ARTHUR, I DIDN'T ASK YOU. *(Pause.)* Don't stick around.

JARED: I don't have anybody else.

RUTH: Me neither.

JARED: You said you have a son…

RUTH: Had one. You leave now.

JARED: Died? *(Deducing.)* No…

RUTH: Left your age.

JARED: Why.

RUTH: Shhh. His father (Viciousviciousvicious….)

JARED: Have you ever seen him since?

RUTH: (…Viciousviciousvicious.) CAN'T. I CAN'T FIND HIM.

JARED: He must want to hear from you, that's been a long time—

RUTH: SHUSH UP! Matthew's gone he's gone. Arthur said throw him out throw that deviant OUT he's OUT OF THIS HOUSE TONIGHT and, and I, I… *(At Arthur's gravestone.)* You *lay off* with the curses, LAY OFF with those daggers daggers daggers in my ears.

JARED: Hey, woah…

RUTH: Daggers in my heart…

JARED: Look, I gotta—

RUTH: Maybe he *is* dead.

JARED: *No,* he's not dead. You hear me? I'm talking to you…

RUTH: I'm looking at you. Your eyes…

JARED: What…

RUTH: Will you look at your eyes. You have his eyes. My eyes. My dear darling boy. Do you know him?

JARED: He's…he's okay.

RUTH: Good. Matthew doesn't know what happened to me. I slid. I kept sliding. I liked it.

JARED: He doesn't need to know.

RUTH: Won't he ever come back?

JARED: He can't.

RUTH: The house is still there, it's just I left it a while ago. Should I go back? Should I hope?

JARED: No.

RUTH: Won't he ever forgive me?

JARED: *(Pause.)* No.

RUTH: What did I do?

JARED: Nothing.

RUTH: Right. Nothing. Move on?

JARED: Yes.

(They stand together.)

Thomas

THOMAS: *(On a pay phone holding a torn front page from the phone book, shreds of other pages stuck to it and fluttering.)* I was with them a couple weeks ago in the café we go to every week after community centre? And it's called, ummm, Reno's. And but it wasn't breakfast and it wasn't lunch yet but we got the same table she always gives us and I sit against the wall. And then she stood on the counter with pink chalk and she started writing on the blackboard. "Try our tasty..." And then a customer jangled the door open and so she had to get down and smear the dust on her apron. "Try our tasty." She got the man coffee and he just sits in his suit and *smokes* and *watches* us. And Robert's being a dope, he's singing and doing this thing with his spoon because Antonia took his fork and knife away and he's thumping, and Antonia's cleaning up Stan who hasn't even started to eat and he's already drooling. And I think what I always think: CAN'T HE JUST SWALLOW? And this man, he wasn't taking little looks, he was watching like crazy. She came over, with the coffee? And I took a refill because I drink a lot of coffee. I have to, it's a habit. But we weren't ready to order, and so she looked at ME like I'm STUPID and plopped me two more creamers and got back on the counter. "...Tasty...tuna melt." Stan ends up having a seizure but he just stays in his chair, Antonia didn't even put him on the floor, which you're supposed to do. And Robert's such a dope with the spoon on the table louder and louder, YAAAAAH!!! And Greg's rocking rocking rocking... The man is watching us, he's...looking. No he's not, he's STARING, and it's NOT POLITE TO STARE, YOU KNOW. And she's right up there pretending nothing's going on. You could see her legs, she had a skirt on. She's writing really pretty: "with a bowl of our soup of the day. $5.90." Are you listening? *(Looks at the page.)* 'Cause you're supposed to listen to me, right?... This IS a crisis! Well if you would just LET me get to the POINT.... See? Stan is finished the seizure but he didn't pee his pants like he normally does? And Antonia takes MY napkin to use to clean up his mouth. Five-ninety. Hmm. The man looks RIGHT AT ME like he could...like he could if I was blind? So I look back at him. I CAN READ, YOU KNOW. I have my OWN ROOM with my OWN PHONE and I have a RADIO that plays tapes. The cook shouts and the waitress jumps down and puts the pink chalk in a little apron pocket and pats her hair. Serves the man eggs. She walks over to us and asks what'll it be. Antonia says scrambled eggs, and everybody else says "scrammled eggs, scrammled eggs, scrammled eggs and toast, toast, toast—toast toast toast..." RETARDS! THESE ARE RETARDS!! I look up at her but she's looking at Egg Man, who's staring at all of us. There's light in her hair and pink dust glowing in her head. She was beautiful. "I would like the tasty s-special please." That's what I said. That's what I said. What? Transferred? I don't want to be transferred!

No! *(He wrenches the box from his pocket and shakes it vigorously.)* No! Nooooo! I am TRYING to tell you something! *(He slams down the telephone.)*

retrieval

(Grass, a view. HUGH, hung over, sits on part of the newspaper. A notebook on the ground a distance from him. HUGH is on his cellular phone, finishing a cigarette.)

HUGH: THINK about it?—Christ, what's there to— Barb, I'm talking HALF AN HOUR! I haven't talked to you in months and there's some things... *(Pause.)* It *won't* get personal—no, no we won't GET INTO—NO—I'm asking you, please, to, to HELP me, Barb. *(Pause.)* A month's grace, that's all I'm— *No,* then you'll get a cheque for two months' support, promise. Well the kid's not gonna starve, is he! Barb—Barb listen, yesterday the bastards, they, they... Okay, can I, can I—wait, just—how's Martin doing. Good, good. He's a good kid isn't he. And you? Okay I KNOW, you're busy. I'm sorry. I'll call you tonight at the house to, to—Hello? Hello?! FUCK!

(PAULA has rushed in, on bike if possible, out of breath, with a bag. HUGH shifts, pretending someone is still on the line.)

YES! I'll have the deal cinched in a week.

(PAULA quickly searches around and finds the notebook; a wave of relief overcomes her.)

My pleasure. Gotta run. Ohhh-kay, Ohhh-kay, right-o. Ciao. *(Hangs up, puts the phone in his coat pocket.)*

PAULA: *(Over HUGH's "conversation".)* Oh hallelujah, thank you God, oh thank you thank you thank you!

(She kisses the book and flops down in giddy, breathless relief. To HUGH:)

I've been looking everywhere. Oh, the relief.

HUGH: Let me guess: is that yours?

PAULA: *(Breathless, out of shape.)* I can't believe I left it here. I know it's only ink and paper but this journal is my LIFE. I'm lost without it.

(She brings out the water bottle from her pack and guzzles. She sees HUGH watching her, falters.)

Want some?

HUGH: Please.

(She passes it.)

PAULA: I never ride bikes, but today? I had to steal my roommate's and backtrack. I totally dreaded that somebody on the bus found it this morning and would, like, be reading it? I just kept thinking "Oh please please please God let it be any place but the bus."

HUGH: Yeah, the bus would be bad.

PAULA: You probably never even ride the bus.

HUGH: Never. I drive or get driven.

PAULA: Wow, so what are you doing up here?

HUGH: *(Fixing a look at PAULA.)* What's your name.

PAULA: Paula.

HUGH: So you came up here this morning?

PAULA: Yeah, I took the bus up just to, you know, look. Sunrise.

HUGH: You saw the sunrise?

PAULA: Yeah. You could see all these people in the houses down there getting up, turning on the lights and the heat and the coffee, rubbing their eyes a little more wrinkled…

HUGH: Ready to meet the day.

PAULA: The real reason is because starting today guess what I'm doing.

HUGH: *(A slight laugh.)* I don't know…

PAULA: Well guess.

HUGH: A job.

PAULA: Sort of, yeah.

HUGH: Well I'd say…I don't know, that you were going to be a writer.

PAULA: That's right! How did you guess?!

HUGH: You've got poet's hands.

PAULA: *(Self-conscious, she sits on her hands, which are chapped and red with eczema.)* Poet's hands—well that's a good start, right? Hey! *(Retrieving a handbill from her pack.)* I have my first reading tonight—you should come.

HUGH: I should.

PAULA: You ever been there?

HUGH: Don't think so.

PAULA: It's a pretty happening place. Sort of a big coffeehouse, but they serve drinks too, I mean alcoholic. I mean, the drinks are alcoholic, or they, they can be, if you want. I've gone a couple times, to watch. They've got a stage and a mic and lights on you and everything. It's…it's pretty good. Anyways, you must be busy, right?

HUGH: Well…

PAULA: Yeah. *(Pointing to the handbill.)* See my name?

HUGH: What do you write about.

PAULA: Oh! Mostly myself…just, you know…stuff that happened. Experiences.

HUGH: You don't make any of it up? No fantasies?

PAULA: *(Giggling.)* No…

HUGH: You had lunch?

PAULA: What? Um, are you saying…you want—

HUGH: I'm saying—

PAULA: You're saying you're, um—

HUGH: Yes.

PAULA: No. I mean, sorry. I don't like…I don't eat with other people. *(Deflecting.)* Gosh, wow…you know you wouldn't think the grass'd be dry this time of year? Guess 'cause we're on top of a hill, the water can drain off.

HUGH: It doesn't.

PAULA: Huh?

HUGH: Wait till you stand up, your skirt'll be wet.

PAULA: Oh. No, I think I found a dry spot here. *(Checking herself.)* No, well, no, I think that's just normal, I think that's, you know, like grass-dampness.

HUGH: Must've been wet up here this morning. *(Spreads out part of the newspaper for her to sit on.)* Dewy. So you took the bus…

PAULA: *(Of newspaper.)* Thanks. Yeah, practically the crack of dawn, just some like, you know, people at the front off to their, whatever, community centre? And there was just like me at the back and this one guy, empty aisle between us. He had this totally…oh I don't know, scary leather jacket with his hair all… *(Gestures.)* and these baby-squashing boots.

HUGH: Really…

(HUGH's cellular phone rings. Silence.)

PAULA: Aren't you going to get that?

HUGH: Thinking about it.

PAULA: Who is it? *(Waiting.)* Your wife?

HUGH: *(Removing his coat.)* Divorced.

PAULA: Work? Somebody from work?

(HUGH aggressively balls up his coat and sets it at a distance, glaring at it. Pause. The ringing finally stops. He remains focussed on the coat, a dangerous edge to him.)

HUGH: *(Of PAULA's story.)* So this guy…

PAULA: Right. Something had happened to him. And I swear I'm not making this up, but he was…talking. His nose was against the window and he was sort of huddled against his reflection mumbling. Weird, eh? I thought only old people talked to themselves.

HUGH: What did he say.

PAULA: You couldn't hear.

HUGH: Did you want to?

PAULA: Well sure. Because he was so intense.

HUGH: Where'd he get off.

PAULA: And *then* he would *look* at me—

HUGH: You were looking at him. Which stop—

PAULA: Because he was looking at *me*!

HUGH: *Which stop.*

PAULA: Don't know, past here. I got off first.

HUGH: Hm… You give him a name?

PAULA: Like make one up?

HUGH: Yeah: say *(Guttural.)* Barry. You just *know* what a Barry looks like. Or *(Lisps.)* Bruce. Or Philip.

PAULA: People are named those names.

HUGH: It's not cruel. Try it: give me a name.

PAULA: *(Considers.)* Hugh.

HUGH: Hugh. *(Pause.)* You guessed right.

PAULA: NO WAY! OH MY GOD!

HUGH: Quite a skill you've got there…

PAULA: This is so weird! Talk about a connection!

HUGH: I was thinking that myself.

PAULA: Huh.

(He is close to her.)

HUGH: I bet you look through windows.

PAULA: *(Scoffing.)* Yeah?

HUGH: No, I mean when you're walking down the street.

PAULA: Like window shopping?

HUGH: At night, when you're feeling low and lonely and you go for a walk, don't you look into people's windows? Glance through the blinds of a basement apartment, hope to…catch something inside.

PAULA: I never walk at night. *(Beat.)* What do you see.

HUGH: You're curious.

PAULA: It's…it's a professional interest.

HUGH: Mostly nothing: people cooking, the cluster of a dinner party…maybe someone in his underwear ironing or dancing around the living room.

PAULA: What happens if they see you.

HUGH: It's night, they can't see out. They're mostly watching TV anyway. Whole apartment blocks, windows flickering grey and white.

PAULA: Then why do you do it.

HUGH: We all do it. You know why.

PAULA: What, like sex?

HUGH: To see a person, really naked. The way I see you.

PAULA: How do you…

HUGH: The way you are when you think no one is watching.

PAULA: You're not supposed to see those things. People keep their curtains closed so you don't—

HUGH: Well that's the thing: sometimes you don't close the curtains, sometimes you actually want the chance to be seen. Maybe it gives you one person in the world: you'll never meet, but he understands you. Like you with the guy on the bus you were staring / at.

PAULA: I was *not staring. (Beat.)* Look, I should go.

HUGH: Let's have lunch.

PAULA: You don't even know me.

HUGH: I do. We like the same things.

PAULA: No we DON'T.

(Creeped out, PAULA moves away. About to leave, she stops.)

It was his eyes, these intense eyes were why I was looking at him.

HUGH: And his cheekbones.

PAULA: His—sure, yeah…

HUGH: And the cords in his long soft neck, you liked that?

PAULA: No. How do you—

HUGH: You didn't like that?

PAULA: It wasn't— It was his spirit.

HUGH: And the "thin love in his empty arms…"

PAULA: *(Beat.)* The…what?

HUGH: "...Ready to wrap around a soul like mine"?

PAULA: Oh my God...

HUGH: *(Smiling.)* Well those were the words you used.

PAULA: You read it!

HUGH: It's good stuff—

PAULA: You asshole! I can't believe you—

HUGH: What are you ashamed of? You want to be a writer.

PAULA: These are...exercises. In description.

HUGH: You'd do the same if you found—

PAULA: If I found a book I'd take it and call the person. I would not leaf through it like it was, was pornography and leave it in the dirt for somebody else to find!

HUGH: I never thought I'd meet you!

PAULA: Well you did.

HUGH: You know, when you see somebody naked it's never as you expect. It's either worse or it's better but it's never what you expect. *(He takes out a page he'd torn from the journal.)* "His face pressed against the window..."

PAULA: That's mine!

HUGH: "...His bleary eyes seize the scene rushing by...."

PAULA: Shut up!

HUGH: *(But he continues, clearly impressed by her words.)* "He dreams of his heart's borrowed address / and wonders how he'll pay for it. / In this city nobody can afford to own anything."

PAULA: *(Pause. Struck by his recital.)* Yeah.

HUGH: You've got a perceptive imagination—

PAULA: I am a normal person!

HUGH: Who desires. I know what you want, what you'd like to have done to you. I know your body from that book. His too. You made him…beautiful.

PAULA: *(Beat.)* I made you want him.

HUGH: *(Scoffs, unsettled.)* What?

PAULA: When you read that poem in there? You wanted him.

HUGH: No…

PAULA: WHAT then.

HUGH: I want you, your…your…

PAULA: SAY IT. *(Derisory.)* What, my BODY?

HUGH: Your spirit. To be close to it, to take it and squeeze its softness. *(He stands close to PAULA.)* My hand. Please?

PAULA: *(Trembling.)* You want it?

HUGH: Yes.

(PAULA kicks him in the balls: hard, swift and crippling. Wailing in pain, HUGH crumples into a heap, fetal position, on the ground. PAULA shrinks back, astounded by herself.)

PAULA: You scumbag asshole, I hope you die. *(PAULA grabs her things.)* You ambushed my writing, mocked my poem, laughed at me…. Well what're you gonna tell people now, huh? *(She grabs back the page, victorious.)* It's mine. The story's mine now.

Ruth

(Comfortable residential area, chirping birds. RUTH stands with her bags, one with JARED's flowers poking out, at the front door of her house, a pile of flyers and newspapers against it. She shouts at the door.)

RUTH: "I'm home!"
Aw leave off, pickin' on me, Arthur. Pick, pick, pickin'.
You wanna know the truth? *(Sizing up the house.)*
It's bad.
It's not just slugs and squeaky doors anymore.
Place's a pile of junk.
Stucco's falling into your lawn, into hundreds of dandelions, crazy heads going to seed
and blowing away, blowing away.

(She spins around, a long suspicious gaze at us, at the houses across the street.)

They're watchin' me, Husband.
Shushin' back the curtains, peering out from their dark little homes.
(viciousviciousvicious)

I never loved you, Arthur.
I only figured that out after the fact.
Vicious circle started day after you were in the ground.
Cold snap, three inches of snow and it was still coming down. But by Jehovah, no way
I was shovellin' that, not now.
Matthew should've been out there, out shovellin'.

RUTH: *(cont'd)* Next morning I look out, cruel blue sky, vicious cold.
All the neighbours've shovelled their strip of sidewalk out front, but oh-ho, nobody did mine. They stopped at the line, by the book.
I'll wait: sun'll melt it, or it'll rain the snow away.
But by noon, 'sa strip of dead glass in front of the house, people slippin' by.

Kids'll be walkin' past goin' home from school soon!
Little shoes slippin',
So I try, Arthur, I take your shovel out there, scrape till my arms ache but the tool just skids over.

Okay. I could borrow some kitty litter: Mrs. Gallagher next door.
Knock and stand there puffing: "Please could you help me? Just a cup or two? For traction."
What would she say—NO?
SHUSH IT! I KNOW she'll say yes, Arthurrr, she'll squeeze out one of her sweet putrid smiles, have me wait dripping snow and sweat and snot on her welcome rug while she measures litter into a zip-lock bag for me to spread on the ice in front of my house.

No. I won't. I won't do that.
'Cause I know you, Gallagher, you'll dine out on it. You'll be the one who HELPED me, the authority: "Oh Ruth's slipping. The house is just too much for her, can't even handle the bloody sidewalk." HA HAA. Well Matthew would've been here with me if it weren't for, for…
Bitches. I can hear you cackling. See you behind your windows! *(Rising panic.)* Your brittle hair, your tiny pink tongues and the way you OBEY! Can smell your terror and regret, wobbling over your sinks and garden beds.
All the failures, all the failing you did for your husbands.
You're the ones who are CRAZY!

(Exhausted, she flops against the door. She absently picks up some of the newspapers and put them into a bag. She looks in the mail slot low on the door.)

Petrified mouse shit on the rugs, scads of scratch pads and fridge magnets realtors slipped through the mail slot.
Bills. Bills, eh?
(A quiet call.) Anything still on in there?

(She listens.)

No Arthur, I don't mean you.

(She reaches down her neck and from within the layers of her clothing, retrieves two keys on a rope around her neck. She takes it off and holds it.)

That night after the snow I sat alone in the front room, lights off like the place was empty.
I waited for people to walk past, slip around the ice and curse.
They cursed me… I heard them.
I heard what you said about me!
And me, I cursed you, Arthur.
Said your name, cursing your fresh grave and the snow on it.
You weren't worth it.
Matthew's not coming back.
Shush. Please Arthur, no more.

(She slips the key through the mail slot.)

rood

(Church. Pews. Light streams through stained glass windows, suffusing the air with golden thickness. LONNIE, now with a leather case, sits in one pew. The newspaper spilling out of her bag, PAULA sits in the pew behind her. LONNIE looks at the altar, only vaguely interested in the stranger behind her.)

PAULA: "Poet's hands", that's what he said. Thing is, I actually have this, this sort of rash on my hands, and feet? They don't know why. Ugly. When I was a kid, in school? I couldn't help picking at it. They were always bleeding. People made fun of me. Poet's hands. Hope he's right.

(PAULA crawls over the pew to sit next to LONNIE.)

So even though he was all weird, I thought, there's something about this guy. 'Cause of what he said about my hands. So. I kissed him.

(LONNIE turns to regard PAULA fully.)

LONNIE: I thought he was threatening you.

PAULA: He was but I called his bluff.

LONNIE: You're alone with this guy on top of a hill, he propositions you, and then you *kiss* him?

PAULA: What, you think I'm lying to you?

LONNIE: No, it's just that he could have attacked you.

PAULA: Well he didn't, okay? You shouldn't insinuate I'm lying. I just met you, why would I lie to you.

LONNIE: Right.

PAULA: So I kissed him and then I touched his, his, his face, I touched his face, and boom, he...guess what: he fainted.

LONNIE: Fainted?

PAULA: Yes! True blue human contact was too much. So guess what I did.

LONNIE: You didn't.

PAULA: I did!

LONNIE: What!

PAULA: I gave him mouth-to-mouth.

LONNIE: You gave him mouth-to-mouth?

PAULA: Yes! What else was I supposed to do!

LONNIE: Shh.

(They look around the church.)

PAULA: I mean *I* didn't know it was only a faint—it looked like he'd stopped breathing. He might've had a heart attack or something. So I'm giving him mouth-to-mouth and actually it's not too bad, you know? And then guess what he did.

LONNIE: He came to.

PAULA: He, he...he CAME.

LONNIE: Shh! —What?!

PAULA: Right in his pants. I'm, you know, resurrecting him—

LONNIE: —Resuscitating him—

PAULA: —Yeah and bam, an orgasm shoots him back to consciousness.

LONNIE: *(Weighing the possibility.)* I've never heard of this.

PAULA: It's pretty common. I mean, not to me, but I've read about it.

LONNIE: Where.

PAULA: I can't remember. *(Beat.)* Well in the Bible for one thing, when Jesus brings people back to life.

LONNIE: It doesn't say that.

PAULA: Or when angels touch you: bam, you have an orgasm. What's that word…

LONNIE: That's not in the bible!

PAULA: …ECSTASY.

LONNIE: That is utterly different.

PAULA: You think I'm making this UP?

LONNIE: *No*, I didn't say that…

PAULA: I mean, I know it's strange, but sometimes strange things happen. Don't strange things ever happen to you?

LONNIE: Sure.

PAULA: Right.

LONNIE: Then what.

PAULA: Then I left him, ecstatic in the grass, wet spot in his pants.

LONNIE: So you fought back.

PAULA: *(Scoffs.)*

LONNIE: Really, you had the swift, self-assured confidence to, to stand up, hit the guy right where it counts. A kiss: his weak spot: exactly what he wanted. Exactly what he was terrified of.

PAULA: *(Back-pedalling.)* I didn't really do anything.

LONNIE: Sure you did. It's odd, but it's, well, it's very… empowered.

PAULA: No, it's not, it's—

LONNIE: You probably touch people like that every day.

PAULA: I don't! I work in the library checking out books, okay? When you're behind a counter most people don't even look at you. I mean, they might watch how fast I can sign out a book, which is really fast, *especially* with them all GAWKING at my ECZEMA. Anyways...I came in here to just...think it over, give thanks. What were you praying for?

LONNIE: *(Almost embarrassed.)* Well I wasn't "praying"...

PAULA: It's nothing to be ashamed of.

LONNIE: Just trying to sort a few things out.

PAULA: Day off?

LONNIE: Called in sick.

PAULA: What's your job?

LONNIE: I work in radio.

PAULA: I love the radio! I always have it on. So, nobody ever recognises you, huh?

LONNIE: No.

PAULA: Hey—do you know that woman, the angel of the bridge?

LONNIE: No.

PAULA: Come on, you do, you're just sworn to secrecy, right?

LONNIE: No. Her show will be on another station.

PAULA: I wonder if I know her. They said on the news that she was a janitor.

LONNIE: Bank teller.

PAULA: Right, okay. Hey! What are you doing tonight? I mean, you want to come see me read my poetry? I'm just the, you know, the warm-up act, but it should be really good. You should come.

(Gives her a handbill.)

PAULA: *(cont'd)* I'm on early, so don't be late.

LONNIE: I'll try.

PAULA: See? That's my name there: Paula. I'll dedicate a poem to you. Um, you know what? You've got this…I can see a… *(Pause. PAULA finally touches her own cheekbone.)*

(LONNIE races for her compact.)

Blotch.

(Her face in the compact, LONNIE performs maintenance.)

Oh. *(Silence. PAULA has messed up again.)* Make-up, eh? Always got to touch it up.

LONNIE: Right.

PAULA: So what happened—

LONNIE: You know, people aren't actually supposed to *talk* in here.

PAULA: Sorry. *(Beat.)* Well there's nobody else in here. I mean, who could hear us? *(Silence. They both look toward the altar.)* Whoo. So do you need a place to stay tonight?

LONNIE: *(Slight laugh.)* Oh no, I'm fine… I have a place I'm staying.

(In the next lines LONNIE takes a tube of hand lotion from her purse.)

PAULA: Where?

LONNIE: Well I haven't actually booked it yet.

PAULA: But you've got friends, right?

LONNIE: *(Flustered, she squeezes out too much lotion.)* Damn.

PAULA: Here.

(PAULA takes some of the lotion with her own hands. The lotion-management makes the women laugh.)

Well if you can, come to my reading, okay?

LONNIE: I'll sure try.

(For a while, their four hands are intertwined in a washing motion, applying the lotion on each other. LONNIE becomes fascinated by PAULA's hands.)

PAULA: Do you think I'm too plain for someone, like, normal to want to be with?

LONNIE: *(Awkward laugh.)* You're not plain.

PAULA: Right. I know the first thing you thought when you saw me.

LONNIE: What.

PAULA: Ugly as sin. Fat.

LONNIE: What's the first thing you thought about me.

PAULA: Beautiful.

LONNIE: See how wrong we were?

(They sit caressing each other's hands. LONNIE looks around the church. PAULA impulsively takes LONNIE's face in her hands. Both are moved by such rare tenderness. With a scabby, greasy hand, PAULA smooths away the make-up from LONNIE's cheek, revealing the bruise. LONNIE lets her.)

PAULA: Such a beautiful face.

(LONNIE kisses PAULA, fully.

Intermission.)

Lonnie

(Sound of tape rewinding. Lights come up on LONNIE, who sits alone in a confessional with her case and the newspaper, rewinding her mini cassette recorder. She then speaks into it.)

LONNIE: A p.s. to the note I left: look, I'm sorry. All I took today were two suitcases with my clothes. I've stored them somewhere. That's it, *(Looking at the case.)* just a few other things. You're getting more than your fair share, Dirk, so just forget about coming after me. Don't bother calling me at work, I'm going to t-tell reception to, to…

(Stops recording, rewinds. Looks out: nobody. Starts.)

Hi scumbag. Miss me yet? You'd never guess where I am.

(Stops, rewinds. Starts.)

It's me. I want to tell you about this sort of dream I had this morning. I was dead. But I could see everything. Everyone was there: there'd been those midnight calls you can only make when somebody dies, when you're forgiven, even thanked for your trouble. Word spread because in my will there was a phone tree. And this phone tree stretched out backward through my life into every nook, reaching everyone I've never been able to forget. People took the week off, dashed to the airport, paid exorbitant prices for a ticket, they didn't care, and they're landing and strangers, they just recognise each other— "Are you going to Lonnie's service?" People pick them up, give them a ride, a place to stay. Put them up in their homes.

In the church there was this massive photograph of my face projected on the back wall and an ocean of flowers, and a flickering mountain of candles. There was this…show of my life. People got up and recounted the major episodes like acts in a play.

And you're there. You get on stage. I'm floating above the packed congregation and you look up and WHAM, you look right at me. But you can't see me. You just look so very, very sorry, for everything you'd ever done to me.

And then you begin to cry, you do, you cry in front of these people.

Because you killed me.

You look out and ask yourself the same questions everyone is asking, staring at that huge photo of me: "Is this Lonnie? Lonnie knew all these people?" They realise, each one of them, they *didn't really know who I was*. And so they cry.

You'll be home in a few hours, you'll get yourself a drink. Sink's clean, fridge full, everything in place. Then you'll notice the empty hangers in the closet or the frail page on the dining room table, pen lying across it at a careful angle. And you'll sit down with your drink and you'll read it.

You have no idea what I'm capable of. You know what I just did? I met somebody. A stranger, in the city. Who'd think it would be so easy. She wants me to see her tonight, Dirk, I'm going someplace to meet her, and then I'm going to take her and we're going to, we're going to…

(Stops recording.) What. An accident. A glorious accident, that's all it was.

(Starts recording.) Like after my service some of those people would meet for the first time and go home together and have sex, just to prove that they are still alive. They'll create something—pleasure in another body—with a virtual stranger. They're crazy, they're saying yes to it and it opens up and

LONNIE: *(cont'd)* flows again, this terrible, painful flow, in and out. They need to feel the old wound bleed again, they need this suffering, yes, this wonderful relentless desperate vast aching loneliness, to have it held like a stunned bird, warmed back to life by tender hands. Love will be made that day. It's the most perfect, precisely perfect day, a day of unbelievable joy and perfection.

(She clicks off the recorder.)

Only I'm not there. I won't be there.

(Sits.)

deliver

(Street outside library. Traffic. Mailbox. Woman's wallet on the ground. JARED stands on the corner, trying to hustle his first trick. His hair is now conventionally styled and he wears his own soft cotton clothes.

JARED sees the wallet a distance from him. He looks around: nobody notices. Stares. Goes to it. Waits, thinking. Picks it up. Looks around. Furtively opens it. Pulls out the money, $200, crisp bills. Stares at his hands. Looks around. Goes to the mailbox, opens the slot. Stops, reconsiders.

THOMAS enters carrying library books. He spots JARED.)

THOMAS: Hello.

(JARED spins around, sees him and lets the wallet slide into the mailbox, pocketing the money.)

Mailing something?

JARED: Yeah. *(He composes himself and gets back to hustling.)*

THOMAS: I got a letter. (*Of library.*) They asked me to leave in there. Most places you can go in the day you're not allowed to talk. Like churches and galleries. *(The pet box is under his coat, over his heart. He surreptitiously checks and pokes it periodically.)* Libraries. *(He watches JARED nervously hustle.)* I saw you before. You had all that, you know... *(Mimes hair.)*

JARED: Yeah.

THOMAS: How come you changed?

JARED: Weren't my clothes.

THOMAS: Whose were they? *(Pause.)* "Tide's in, dirt's out." Aren't you early?

JARED: For what.

THOMAS: For what you're doing.

JARED: *(Suddenly unsure.)* I don't know, I've never done this.

THOMAS: Don't worry, I seen people come by. Rush hour, right? People coming out from work... *(Of book.)* Look at the cover on this one. You know snakes? Know their skins? You know what they do?

JARED: Look, I'm...busy right now.

THOMAS: Right.

(JARED returns to cruising.)

See, he loosens the skin at the lips and takes it takes it takes it back wider and wider. Crawls out of the hole, out of his old skin, turns it inside out. Comes out of his old mouth like a s-scream. They don't know why. Thing is, I got a letter last week. Written to me, my name right on the envelope. I didn't hardly know what to do! *(Laughs.)*

JARED: Look guy, could you just take your books and...

THOMAS: *(Lips pursed, THOMAS flashes JARED his library card.)* My card.

(JARED stares, confounded.)

I can read. *(Beat.)* There was one page inside the envelope. Just tissue paper. When you hold it up, you can see the light 'cause there's these little nips from where the pen cut through it. She just picked me, it's weird.

(JARED continues hustling, trying to ignore him.)

She could've picked anybody. She could've picked you even. But she picked me, out of everybody.

You should hear this letter. It's in my pocket. I think I should maybe read it to you.

(JARED looks at THOMAS.)

It's not long. *(Holds it up.)* See?

JARED: Whatever.

THOMAS: I don't think she'd mind. *(Shaking his head at the envelope.)* Tsk tsk tsk. Look: there's no postal code. *(He reads flat, haltingly.)* "Dear Mr. Thomas Bailey:" Me. "You may remember me from the café. You gave me your number." See, I gave her my number 'cause I have my own phone—

JARED: Yeah yeah.

THOMAS: Right, um... "...number. After I finish this letter and take it downstairs to the post box, I'm going to come back up to my apartment and take thirty tablets of monamine oxidase inhibitor. I should be dead by supper time. Nobody will know I am dead and I don't want to surprise the landlord a month from now. So could you please phone the police and tell them."

JARED: Holy...

THOMAS: "Also tell them not to break down the door because I will leave it unlocked. Sorry to be a bother, but I didn't know who else to ask. Thanking you in advance, Margaret Sokolchoff, 12–4571 Fraser Street."

JARED: Holy...

THOMAS: I know!

JARED: Did you call?

THOMAS: No.

JARED: What? When did you get the letter?

THOMAS: I didn't think things were ready.

JARED: What do you mean?

THOMAS: Everybody's gonna rush into her apartment and mess everything up. I think she's a tidy person and right now it must be so peaceful.

JARED: Look: give me the address—

THOMAS: You can't call.

JARED: I'll call the police for you.

THOMAS: (*Upset.*) She wants me to do it.

JARED: What was her name—give me her name.

THOMAS: Why didn't she just write earlier—

JARED: Can I see the letter?

THOMAS: ...to say she was really sad, and would I help her.

JARED: People don't ask for help like that.

THOMAS: Why didn't she phone my *number* instead.

JARED: People don't do that!

THOMAS: Why? I w-would have answered.

JARED: She'd made up her mind. I know—

THOMAS: But how long is it between making up your mind and doing it? Not very. If you just take long enough you change your mind.

JARED: Just call and get it over with.

THOMAS: I used to go to her café after community centre. She was the waitress.

JARED: Where.

THOMAS: Reno's.

JARED: *(Pause.)* What'd she look like.

THOMAS: Normal. Glasses, curly brown hair. She wore skirts.

JARED: Could you...tell anything?

THOMAS: No.

JARED: Okay, this is crazy. Don't get sucked in, just make the call.

THOMAS: The thing is, I got this letter, from a person. I could've helped her. But I couldn't do that even.

JARED: Man, what *is* it today?! Listen. Tom—Tim… Tim.

THOMAS: Tom…*mas*.

JARED: I know what this feels like, Tom. It's not your fault.

(Glum, THOMAS begins to exit.)

Hey! Tom, wait, I'd like to…I could help you. I could be with you when you phoned.

THOMAS: I don't want to phone.

JARED: Wait! Okay, we could go visit her. You've got her address, the apartment's unlocked. We could just see her. That way you could make sure she was ready and then, then…we could phone.

THOMAS: We can't do that…

JARED: Sure we can. We could go right now.

THOMAS: I wreck everything.

JARED: We can help her.

THOMAS: I love her.

(He hands JARED the letter.)

She'll die if I open the door.

chicken

(Park, by a pond, dusk. Leaves. LONNIE sits on a bench with her purse and case beside her, poring over the newspaper, circling classified apartment rental ads. RUTH stands with her bags around her, one with JARED's wilted flowers poking out. From one bag she pulls hunks of bread, throwing them downstage or into the audience. Sound of ducks intensify when they are fed.)

RUTH: Here chickie chickie chickie…come on, close up to Mama. *(Smacking noises.)* Now don't fight, plenty to go around. No—hey you, *hey* you, hey! You leave him alone. Always pickin' on the little ones, pickin' pickin'…pick… Here little one, *(Throwing far but not far enough.)* no no, don't be afraid, come in closer. *(Throwing large clumps to an area near her.)* You bullies, nip at the little one, now he's too afraid to come in close. *(Throwing far but not far enough. She looks out, worried about the little duck.)* Poor thing must be starving. *(Quiet.)* Come on in, little baby!

LONNIE: *(Reading.)* It's not hungry.

RUTH: *(Scoffing.)* "Not hungry", these chickies're always hungry. *(Throwing out.)* Come on little one, I can't throw that far….

LONNIE: Ducks don't eat bread.

RUTH: "Don't eat bread…" What do you think they're doin' out there?

LONNIE: It isn't good for them. They're birds.

RUTH: What do you mean "they're birds", I know they're birds. Hey! This is the staff of life here. This here's the staff of life!

LONNIE: It swells up in their stomachs.

RUTH: I feed 'em every day. I go to all the bakeries and they give me their old bread. *Every single day.* I do all the ponds in this park—they all quack and splash and eat the bread. I care for them. They know me. *(She feeds them.)* Here chickie, gobble gobble, you just love this bread, don't you, just looove it. *(Concerned look out to the little one.)* Maybe he's hurt. *(Trying to make the throw.)* Blast it, I can't do this anymore.

(RUTH turns to look at LONNIE. LONNIE turns to her paper, RUTH back to feeding.)

Hey. You Miss.

(She proffers the bag. Pause. LONNIE gets up, only to look.)

I'm a bad throw.

LONNIE: You should feed them seeds, or cat food.

RUTH: Cat food?!

LONNIE: The crunchy stuff. It's better for them.

RUTH: How do you know.

LONNIE: Which one.

RUTH: Oh come on, "which one..." *(Aggravated, RUTH feeds those near her. She never asks for favours. Silence but for the ducks. Finally.)* That one.

(LONNIE reaches into the bag and tears off a large hunk of bread.)

Okay wait wait wait. Let me decoy the rest. *(Throwing close.)* Here chickie, here chickie, that's it, come on close. Okay now throw!

(LONNIE throws far.)

That's it! See? Look! Praise Allah!

(LONNIE takes another large piece and throws it.)

RUTH: *(cont'd)* Hey. Hey! You trying to choke it to death?

LONNIE: *You* throw out huge hunks—

RUTH: These guys like it big. He's a little one—you're gonna kill him.

LONNIE: *(Throwing.)* It has to be big if you want it to get that far.

RUTH: You don't know nothin', Miss Creamy-skin. Miss Prissy-lips. Pretty little life. I know who you are: I came from you.

(Silence. In the next lines RUTH finds a knife and a block of cheese from within her bags. Before eating she removes the candy from her mouth and lifts it above her head. She looks up, says a silent grace and begins to eat. When she is done chewing she will pop the candy back in her mouth.)

LONNIE: *(Brushing her hands, packing up.)* It's certainly a big park. Walking around in here I seem to have lost my, uh... [direction]. Can you point me toward downtown?

RUTH: Your little garden adventure's up? *(Kissing sounds.)* Back to your nice cozy hozey?

LONNIE: You know, cheese is expensive.

RUTH: *(Mouth full.)* Good for the bones.

LONNIE: *(Beginning to search for her wallet.)* You get your nutrients cheaper with less fat if you eat other things. Broccoli.

RUTH: I like cheese.

LONNIE: But you can't afford it.

RUTH: *(At her with the cheese and the knife.)* How do you know what I can afford. Huh? You know what I can afford? You don't know nothin' 'bout me so DON'T BOSS! Thinkin' things about me...

LONNIE: Just trying to help...

RUTH: Well don't.

LONNIE: *(To self, searching.)* Can't see a thing…

RUTH: Moon'll come up soon. Chickies get all quiet now. I sit on the bench, watch 'em glide on the pond, trees get darker, taller…

LONNIE: We should leave now.

RUTH: I never leave the park, Chickie, not at night.

LONNIE: Well can you…would you please walk me to the street? There are dangerous areas in here. Don't want to get lost. I helped you.

RUTH: You did not!

LONNIE: Throwing the bread!

RUTH: You helped the bird.

(LONNIE becomes increasingly agitated, searching through her things.)

I'm not going out there. Worst time, everybody rushin' around. Not safe from people's thoughts of you. This is the cruel time. Everybody in the city wants to be somewhere else.

LONNIE: Where the hell is it…

RUTH: Lose something?

LONNIE: I don't know… *(Thinking.)* Okay: Left the church, got a sandwich, juice…juice, I had it leaving there…. What did I do with it? My God. I think I lost my wallet.

RUTH: Just…cancel everything.

LONNIE: If I don't have my wallet I'm…. No. *(Back to searching.)* This is absurd, it's here. I just can't see a damned thing right now.

RUTH: *(She picks up LONNIE's case, feels the weight of it. Softly.)* You'll get sore carrying this.

(LONNIE grabs it back.)

RUTH: *(cont'd)* Stupid things inside: keepsakes.

LONNIE: These are important things.

RUTH: You don't need them out here.

LONNIE: Damn it, why didn't I check into a hotel right away? Drifted around all day like an idiot, I mean, you spent half of it in a *church*, with, with…I mean what the HELL were you THINKING, you stupid, stupid, idiot…

RUTH: You could take over for me if I got sick. If I…leave off.

LONNIE: *(Passing her hands over her body, a tormented caress that is one last desperate check for the leather lump.)* My God. The ticket for my luggage, my clothes at the bus station. Is in the wallet. I don't have anything. I don't have anything.

(Boom.) I have to go back. Time… *(Checking her watch.)* He won't be home yet. The day after he…does this, he comes home late. I'll get there first, I could just…destroy the letter just, just like nothing happened. *(At RUTH.)* I've got to get out of here. I can't leave him like this.

(With her case, she looks at RUTH. Silence. Breath.)

Which way do I go.

RUTH: Call somebody.

LONNIE: There is nobody I can ask!

RUTH: Friends…

LONNIE: Don't you think I've thought about this? Over and over through my address book, asking myself the same question of every entry pencilled in there. Could I ask them? No.

RUTH: Little bird, don't you know what's good for you?

LONNIE: *(Up close and raging.)* Get me out of this park! It's dark and I'm cold and I need to go home! WHICH WAY DO I GO!!

(LONNIE shakes RUTH, who doesn't respond. Finally LONNIE releases her, knocking RUTH over. Disgusted with herself, LONNIE moves away, grabs her things and begins to exit into the growing darkness. RUTH alone.)

RUTH: *(Looks at the rising moon. Howls.)* Owwwww-oooooooooo! *(Calls.)* That's the wrong way. To the aviary, doves and cockatiels. Fluttering heart of the park.

(LONNIE re-emerges.)

(Pointing.) This way, nice busy street, phone by the kiosk. People.

(LONNIE starts to cross.)

Don't go back.

LONNIE: I'm safe there.

(RUTH grabs LONNIE's case. LONNIE stands exhausted and weak.)

Give that to me.

RUTH: You want it?

LONNIE: Give it! *(She lunges at RUTH and is stopped by a $50 bill RUTH holds out in front of her. Real.)* Where did you get that money.

RUTH: Not you. Take it.

LONNIE: What for.

RUTH: Loan. *(Of case.)* This is collateral.

LONNIE: That's my case, it's my life—

RUTH: To make sure you come back tomorrow.

LONNIE: I'll come back, I promise…

RUTH: You will GET IT TOMORROW. I have a plan. Shelter tonight.

LONNIE: Shelter? I'm not going to one of those—

RUTH: Then you'll come back here in the morning. I know a place you can live. (*Quiet.*) Shush, Arthurrrr.

(She sets down the case between them.)

Try one night without it.

LONNIE: *(Looking at the case with a sadness like nostalgia.)* I'm not like you. Whatever happened to you, that's not…

RUTH: Yes it is.

(LONNIE approaches the case.)

What's your name.

LONNIE: Lonnie.

RUTH: What have you forgotten, Lonnie, that you knew when the sun rose on you this morning.

LONNIE: *(Breaking.)* I don't know what else to do.

(RUTH gives her the money.)

RUTH: Move. Move your life. *(Pointing the way out.)* I'll keep calling to you from behind, Lonnie.

(About to exit with only her purse, LONNIE turns back, afraid.)

And you just, you sing out.

(RUTH begins to sing the chorus to "Cockles and Mussels".)

Come on!

(Faltering, LONNIE joins RUTH in singing.)

That's it, come on, you sing out bright. Tomorrow morning, you know where to find me.

(LONNIE leaves singing, her voice rising stronger and stronger in the distance.)

Louder! I want to hear you! You keep singing!

(RUTH dances, singing along.)

Paula

(At microphone, too close. Nervous.)

PAULA: Thank you, thank you.

Whoo. I didn't expect to go on quite so…early.

(Fussing with papers.) Just stall a moment here… So can people hear me? *(Searches the audience, shielding her eyes.)* Huh. So. Just kind of waiting for this…somebody to show up right now and… anyway.

My first poem is about the fact that…there was a guy…uh, who died on me today. He had a kind of heart attack, died in my arms atop Little Mountain at lunch time. Kind of unbelievable, I know. So anyway, I give to you in my reading debut, "The Elegy to Hugh".

(She looks at her pages.) "When you reclined…" *(Pause.)* "When you reclined amid the faded blossoms…" *(She stand there ashamed of her poem, feeling like a ridiculous fool; she can't read this.)* Stupid.

You know when you just miss the bus? I get mad but not for long because I know there's a reason, right? There'll be someone I'll meet on the *next* bus who'll talk to me or give me an idea or maybe, I don't know, fall in love with me. 'Cause fate is good that way, right?

The problem with fate is you can't always tell. I mean, okay, I get on the next bus and I'm looking at everyone on it. And I'm trying to figure out who is the one I'm supposed to, you know…connect with? I start walking down the aisle trying to get people to look at me so I might know whether or not they're the one and I should sit next to them. But all these people looking out the window or staring at a paperback, they're all wrong. So I get to the back of the bus and I wait. I watch every single person who gets on. And when nothing happens I think, well why did I miss that first bus? So then I figure it's because I'll run into somebody where I'm going, and I wouldn't have if I'd made the first bus and been, you know, on schedule? So all day long it's getting bigger and bigger, this expectation I have for someone, anyone, to, you know, come into my life. End of the day I sit in my room. Door's locked, TV's on. I'm more or less safe. That's it. I got gypped again.

(She peers into the audience, blind. Opening her diary.)
This is true: "My heart cracked."

"My heart cracked
but it wasn't blood pouring
over the smoky pews, no sacred
heart removed and raging.
With the slow explosion of a tulip's embarrassed
blossom, my body opened to your caress,
  dangerously,
as a pale breast under the sun.
You must have heard the song
of a full breath taken hungrily
while the stained light spilled
its indifferent colours on us.
In such an unforgiving asylum
your tongue softened my skin,
relaxed my lips into a fluid
song and crack, my heart opened
with the force of an old seed
insistent and blind,
tendrils reaching with audacious faith."

(Silence. Vulnerable, humiliation rising.)

Hello? *(Quiet.)* Lonnie? You there?

Jared

(Park. Clearing. More leaves, litter. JARED is cruising, nervous, trying to find his first trick.)

JARED: I can't do this. I don't even know where I'm supposed to be.
You laughing at me, Phil?
Small-town faggot trying to hustle his first trick?
Rent boy.
To pay the rent.
Should have seen this guy this morning, he was desperate for it.
For me.
If I could only find that guy again.

I found the wallet, sure, a miracle. But it's nowhere near enough.
I'm trying, okay?
I'm not gonna curl up with a bunch of pills, not like you.
Not like her,
naked on the floor. Her body. Hadn't expected that.
Her nightgown: slippery skin beside her, dried puke all over it.
Her eyes were open. Yours weren't. I never saw your eyes like that.

Tom is crying and retching, cleaning up her vomit caked in the sink
and I'm tearing through her closet,
hangers shrieking along the rod.
Her private place.
I bet nobody'd even been in her bedroom before.
Found a nice dress but we couldn't get it on her, she was too… *(Pause.)*

So we covered her with a comforter,
different coloured squares crocheted together like
one my mom made.
She was ready. So we called.

Waiting, I fluffed cushions, aired the place,
tidied magazines like I was expecting guests.
I even watered the plants. Calm. Not like with you.
Did you think about what you would do to me?
Do you know, Phil? Do you know the mess you
made?

We called, two attendants came. One of them was
really cute.
Then the police, gave us hell for moving
everything.
But so what. We knew what she needed.
Least I looked respectable. I stopped wearing your
clothes.
Seemed useless, couldn't smell you in them
anymore.
Police asked me all the questions. Pretty wild story.
And this time, Phil, I was *in control* of the situation.
I'd seen her eyes. I could look into them, to death. It
didn't destroy me.

And if I can do that, I can do this. Because I'm alive.
And you're not.

(He hears the crack of branches. Alert, he goes in.)

strip

(In the darkness the sound of paper and plastic rustling. Sobbing, almost moaning. Moonlight comes up on PAULA, her diary beside her, crying and shoving food into her mouth, junk food—chips, ice cream, cookies—scattered around her. She gorges on pudding, her hands and mouth darkened by it.

Park, on the shore by river or ocean. HUGH has just entered. Bottle.)

PAULA: *(Shocked.)* F-f-fucking…

HUGH: Well!…

PAULA: …You fucking pervert…

HUGH: Who would have figured…

PAULA: Oh Jesus Lord, don't you come near me.

HUGH: Quite a coincidence.

PAULA: Look, Mister, just let me go.

HUGH: *(Inviting her to pass.)* As you approach, I will move to let you pass.

PAULA: Yeah right, I'll get in the woods and you'll follow me.

HUGH: Moon's sure nice on the water down here. Hey?

(He steps toward her.)

PAULA: DON'T MOVE. Don't you take one step closer to me.

HUGH: *(Toeing the diary by her pack.)* Did you tell the story?

PAULA: What.

HUGH: The story: about me and / you—

PAULA: Yeah, it's my story, I told it.

HUGH: And?

PAULA: ...What.

HUGH: Was it *good*?

PAULA: I don't know!

HUGH: Told the truth?

PAULA: Whatever.

HUGH: You embellished, I can tell. I'm honoured. Stories have a way of running away from us, don't they.

PAULA: I have friends showing up any minute.

HUGH: *(Smiling at the lie.)* If I wanted you, don't you think I'd've done something about it by now?

PAULA: *(As HUGH approaches her.)* I'm late for work.

HUGH: Nobody works at this hour.

PAULA: WELL I DO, IGNORAMUS PERVERT. On the telephone.

HUGH: Doing what.

PAULA: Why does someone phone in the middle of the night.

HUGH: ...Sex? You work at one of those—

PAULA: No, you're disgusting.

HUGH: Well then what, death?

PAULA: I volunteer at a crisis line.

HUGH: People call *you*, in the middle of the night?

PAULA: Yes, asshole. I happen to be very good.

HUGH: You don't seem the type.

PAULA: You can't see me. You'd be surprised who they let answer those phones.

HUGH: Well we're chatting now, you and me.

(PAULA moves to leave.)

Hey? Hey? Isn't that what we're doing? Can't we just HAVE A TALK?! Hey? STOP!

(HUGH grabs PAULA who screams. He continues to hold her, tight, screaming as well, longer and louder than she.)

Don't...do that. Do you know what you did to me today?

PAULA: *(Terrified.)* Please...I'm sorry I kicked...

HUGH: Shouldn't you be punished? Hey? Taking an unsuspecting man...

PAULA: Please...let me go.

HUGH: You came down here looking for something.

PAULA: No, I didn't, honest—

HUGH: Why then.

PAULA: The dark, so nobody would see me. I couldn't go home: my roommate...

HUGH: *(Still holding her close.)* Well I saw you. Feeding your face. Shh, we're just talking. I saw a good one tonight. Looked up and saw a man lose his mind, blind rage through the window, tearing through his entire house, smashed his dining room table in half, everything off the walls, the shelves—and I mean *nice* things. I stood on the other side of the street and watched. What was the gift there?

PAULA: I have to go...

HUGH: Was he telling me what *I* should do?

PAULA: ...No...

HUGH: To you?

PAULA: No!

HUGH: What are you doing down here, huh? *(Shakes her hard.)* Huh? You asking for trouble?

PAULA: No, please…

HUGH: WHAT!

PAULA: *(Terrified.)* I've never been with a guy. I'm a, a virgin. Please, don't hurt me. Not here…

HUGH: What do you think I'm going to do: rape you?

(Beat. He lets her go, suddenly sober, horrified.)

My God. You think I'd *rape you…*?

PAULA: *(A lie.)* No.

HUGH: *(Watching PAULA pull herself together.)* You're a stupid cow, out here like this…

PAULA: Shut up.

HUGH: What are you going to do?

PAULA: What are *you* going to do? You're nothing! Come on, go in.

HUGH: What…?

PAULA: You want to die, then die.

(HUGH stares at her.)

How can I tell you to keep living.

(HUGH turns to face the water, watching it in utter despair, trying to muster the courage. He takes a few things from his pockets and carefully places them on the shore. He sees PAULA's notebook nearby.)

HUGH: You don't want this left on the shore: evidence. Take it.

PAULA: Take it in with you.

HUGH: What…?

(PAULA watches mutely. HUGH turns back to face the water. He begins to go in, then stops.)

You know, I saw that same boy riding the bus this morning. He reminded me. When I was in the navy, middle of the night, I'd wake up in my bunk, rows of bodies slowly breathing. Some guy would always be sobbing, quietly, into his pillow. That low moaning that pains the heart to hear. We were only kids. And all I wanted to do, what I struggled against the rest of the night, was to go to that boy and hold him, hold him until he stopped. That's what I wanted to do.

PAULA: Did you ever?

HUGH: No. You cold?

PAULA: Duh.

(HUGH takes off his coat and gives it to her.)

It's wet.

HUGH: I've been sweating, sorry. Tell me something, Paula.

PAULA: What.

HUGH: Tell me something true.

PAULA: Give me your shoes. Your *shoes.*

(HUGH starts taking off his shoes.)

Which would be worse: having a reading where the only people who're there are your friends or having a reading where none of your friends turn up.

HUGH: What happened?

PAULA: I tried to write about this…*thing*, that happened to me today—to *me*, something *real*, something fated.

But I couldn't. It came out of me same as everything does—all these clumsy, homely, fat words.

I want beautiful things. I want a house open to dozens of friends who come by and visit and have such a hard time leaving, and I'm thin and I eat well and every day I spend my happiest time writing fine, perfect poems, imagining possibilities. I know what I want—I think about it all the time. Why can't I get there? *(Puts HUGH's shoes down at a distance. She stands, somehow revived.)* So. I told you something true. *(Slight joke.)* The shoes are so you can't run after me.

HUGH: Right. Good idea.

PAULA: You cold?

HUGH: No.

PAULA: I'd be cold if I were you.

HUGH: Keep writing. I thought what I read in there was good.

PAULA: *(She doesn't leave.)* Hugh? I did make love to somebody today.

HUGH: That's a beautiful thing. *(HUGH looks out at the water, begins to take off his tie.)*

PAULA: She told me she'd be there. I thought it was a beginning.

HUGH: It was.

PAULA: *(Approaching HUGH.)* Here. *(She begins taking off his suit jacket.)*

HUGH: No. You should go.

PAULA: Oh shush up.

(PAULA will take off his tie, shirt, belt and trousers. She doesn't set out to strip him but rather, through the impact of HUGH's speech, finds one slow gesture leading to another.)

HUGH: This suit: look at it. Nine hundred dollars. Put it on yesterday morning, my best one. Wanted to look sharp. I have to invest in good suits, otherwise I look rumpled. The flesh may be weak but the tailor is mighty strong, hey? I'm...I'm ugly, aren't I, that's what my ex-wife used to tell me. I'd say, "Yeah I'm ugly, but I'm also rich, and I'm powerful." And power is attractive, it is. They'd put me on television sometimes, the news. So this meeting. Yesterday. With the higher-ups.

(HUGH grabs PAULA's hand and holds it a moment, examining it lovingly.)

They fired me. Could've knocked me over with a feather.

(PAULA slips out her hand and continues. HUGH explains his tattoo.)

Got that in the navy. A heart, that's what it is, with an arrow through it. All out of whack now, age stretched the ink around.

It's so easy, Paula, it slides so fast... Look at that suit *(A sad rumpled heap beside him.)*: nine hundred dollars and it's ruined, one day out in the city. I loved that suit.

(As she is about to remove his saggy briefs, HUGH shrinks from her and stands shivering.)

Sorry, I just, I don't know...

PAULA: I want to look at you.

HUGH: Well this is me.

PAULA: Yeah.

HUGH: You go now.

PAULA: You're not going to die. *(Moving close.)* You cold yet?

HUGH: Stop it.

PAULA: Tell me your real name.

HUGH: See this little scar? *(Over his sternum.)* You can't really see it now. I had a hole there, divot in my rib cage. Got it from my mother, congenital. A hollow, just skin, bit of flesh and below was the bottom corner of my heart, beating. It was vulnerable for a kid, I always had to be careful something didn't jab in there and kill me. Imagine me, prairie boy with a sunken chest, in the navy. Had to be careful: there's people, you're around people all the time looking at you. They could see it. First thing after I got out, I went and had it fixed. Cost me everything I had. But easy: no more hole. Just...see? Touch it? Right there. Feel that?

(PAULA gingerly places her hand on his sternum.)

Plastic.

(PAULA's touch becomes more assured. True power enters her and HUGH feels it. He slowly falls to his knees, clinging to PAULA's body, finally breaking. In HUGH's coat, PAULA looks down at him, holding her arms out and gently curving them above the crumpled form, upwards as if in prayer—or ecstasy. She looks up.)

clearing

(Park, late. JARED is on the ground, beaten, inert. LONNIE enters, sees him.)

LONNIE: Oh my—

(LONNIE freezes, staring at him. Wonders what to do. Dead? She backs away. He lets out a sigh. She stops. JARED sees her.)

JARED: Hi.

LONNIE: Hello. Are you all right?

JARED: *(Pause.)* Oh. Just fine thanks.

LONNIE: Should I get some help?

JARED: No. *(Trying to get up, wincing in pain.)* I'll live…

LONNIE: I can call the, the—

JARED: Who. Who would you call.

LONNIE: Well can I, should I…help you?

JARED: No.

LONNIE: What happened.

JARED: What do you think happened?!

LONNIE: Did they rob you?

(JARED looks for the money. Gone.)

Least it's only money.

JARED: Easy for you to say.

LONNIE: Let me help you up, we're going to—

JARED: Just leave!

(Pause. From her dwindling stash LONNIE hands JARED ten dollars.)

LONNIE: Here.

JARED: Gee, thanks.

LONNIE: It's all I can spare, sorry.

JARED: Right.

LONNIE: I know how bad this is.

JARED: How would you know.

LONNIE: I'm in a shelter right now. Couldn't sleep there, too depressing, the sorrow in the walls. Started worrying about this woman I met. They wouldn't let me go, but I convinced them. Just for a walk. She's out here. Older, kind of uh... *(Gesture: crazy.)* I got a bad feeling, thought I'd better find her. She's got my things. You seen her?

JARED: No.

LONNIE: *(Bending down to try and clean him.)* Here, let me—

(JARED spits blood, accidentally on LONNIE.)

Oh—is that, that's—

JARED: ...Sorry...

LONNIE: Oh god, I've got blood, on...

JARED: It's not going to kill you!

LONNIE: I know that. Let's have a look at you.

(She gets out Kleenex and with her saliva begins to clean him. He shrinks away, disgusted.)

Hey. Hey.

(She continues to clean away his blood. He lets her.)

JARED: I gotta leave this city, I fucking hate it.

LONNIE: Well what were you thinking, out here?

JARED: I don't know!

LONNIE: You've got to be careful.

JARED: Maybe sometimes I don't *feel* like being careful!

LONNIE: Then you've nobody to blame but yourself.

JARED: It was this kid! He was standing nervous here, in this clearing, in the moonlight trying to attract me. I see him and I know, he's the one. I go to him, touch his…

LONNIE: What.

JARED: His…you know. My legs are trembling. His shaky breath's on my neck. And his hand.

LONNIE: What.

JARED: His hand graced my cheek and boom, I'm thinking, this is the one. I'd been looking for someone to save me, I'd almost given up, and here he is. We'll go home, to my home, and we'll make love, on that bed, and all the bad stuff is over, finally, I should have known. I should have known. Something in his eyes. His need. His shame. It's okay, I said. Kiss.

LONNIE: Decoy.

JARED: Before the forest tore open with shouts, blunt leather boots pounding, pounding, I couldn't breathe, hugging to my gut the boot of one of those boys. It was him, my little Judas. Fuckers.

LONNIE: Fuckers. *(Still cleaning.)* So they got their kicks.

JARED: *(Chuckle.)* Yeah, they got their kicks.

LONNIE: Well you can't trust strangers.

JARED: No.

LONNIE: *(Pause. She continues cleaning.)* So this is the place where um, men…

JARED: Yeah. Least I think so.

LONNIE: Guess I'm safe then.

JARED: I guess. And if any bashers come we'll just start kissing.

LONNIE: ...They'll look over and think, "Oh, now there's two normal people."

JARED: ...Walk on by, leave us alone.

LONNIE: Good plan. *(Finishing cleaning him.)* There.

JARED: How do I look.

LONNIE: Listen to me: nobody's going to save you. You think there's somebody out there, and if you just walk the right path you'll come across him? It won't happen.

JARED: But it does: people, they come into my life, save me....

LONNIE: They don't.

JARED: They do! You know, like the angel of the bridge.

LONNIE: A lie.

JARED: It's not! She saved him, people said—

LONNIE: She didn't save him!

JARED: Well she did *something* to him. What was it? What did she say, to keep him alive?

LONNIE: *(Pause.)* She said, "I've been standing on this bridge with you for three hours, you jerk. You can't jump now, think what it would do to me."

JARED: That's it?

LONNIE: That's it.

JARED: How do you know.

LONNIE: 'Cause the guy got off the bridge. For now. He got down, didn't he. For now. Is that what you want?

JARED: No.

LONNIE: Then save yourself.

candy

(Park. Playground, very late. Swings, more leaves, more litter. RUTH sits on a swing, her bags torn and scattered around her, the bunch of flowers ruined, LONNIE's case nearby. RUTH sits on a swing, wildly tearing through a pile of newspapers section by section in a frenzied imitation of reading. His mouth messy, THOMAS eats from a tub of melted ice cream. Some of his library books are strewn nearby.)

THOMAS: Lucky, eh Ruth?

RUTH: *(Mumbling.)* Gotta get through this news, news, all this news...

THOMAS: They were dumb not to eat it right away.

RUTH: You go home.

THOMAS: It's like soup, see? Like baby food.

RUTH: Should at least phone them.

THOMAS: I could phone my *own* line. Phone myself.

RUTH: Fat lot of good that'd do.

THOMAS: *(Playing.)* "Hello? Hello? Thomas Bailey please." I could get that long-distance feeling.

RUTH: Y'aven't been home in two days.

THOMAS: Don't want to go home. Bunch of retards.

RUTH: Thomas, that's why you're there.

(Silence. THOMAS is hurt. RUTH goes back to the papers, crumpling them up as she finishes them.)

Falling behind.

(THOMAS starts to pick up litter.)

Why're you doing that.

THOMAS: I'm NOT A RETARD!

RUTH: *(Beat.)* You don't need to pick that stuff up.

THOMAS: It's because my Mom died when I was a baby, that's why I'm with them. I'm a ward. Of the...people. Of you. But the p-people who run things now, they're new. They don't know the real reason I'm there, that it's because she died, not because— See, it's because I'm with Stan and Robert and Greg all the time, I can't ever make any other friends. I can't get better. If she didn't die I wouldn't be like this with these, these s-stupid people. *(Gathering litter again.)* That man today who helped me? He thinks I'm a retard. He won't call. "I'm in the book," I said. "Bailey, Thomas. Just look it up in the book and you'll find me there."

RUTH: *(Of his gathering.)* They got people who do that. *(Throwing papers.)* It's their job, leave it.

THOMAS: Well what else am I supposed to do around here?!

RUTH: I bet your snake misses you.

THOMAS: *(Blows up, throwing all the garbage at her.)* How can he MISS me! Next time I see him I'm going to shove my finger down his throat and rip out his guts! I wreck everything!

(He throws the pet box on the ground and crushes it.)

I WRECK EVERYTHING! I was trying to fix it here. She was dead!

RUTH: You told me.

THOMAS: They carried her out of her home. That man, that Jared, he opened that door, he told them everything, like he knew her, they never even looked at me.

RUTH: ...I know, I know...

THOMAS: It was MY JOB to help her, I KNEW her.

RUTH: ...I know...

THOMAS: They took the letter! She gave *me* that letter and they took it and I'm never gonna get it back!

RUTH: *(Gruff.)* Come. Come.

(THOMAS drops at her feet, head on her lap.)

THOMAS: Why am I alive?

RUTH: *(Patting his head.)* Hungry?

THOMAS: No.

RUTH: Want cheese?

THOMAS: Are you tired of me?

RUTH: I'm tired of everybody. Candy?

THOMAS: No.

RUTH: *(Taking a candy.)* Thomas, you helped her along. She chose you.

THOMAS: Out of the book.

RUTH: We're faeries... *(Throwing candy wrappers.)* People fear us, that's all. 'Cause we go anywhere.

THOMAS: *(Getting up.)* Yeah!

RUTH: *(Retrieving copious candy wrappers from her pockets and throwing them around her. Cynically.)* Sprinkling faerie dust.

THOMAS: But Ruth, you're so mean.

RUTH: Oh yeah? Well tomorrow I'm givin' someone a home.

THOMAS: Mom...

RUTH: Draughty box wasn't really mine anyways. Was HIS, all his doing...

THOMAS: Mom.

RUTH: *(She heard.)* Thomas…

THOMAS: What, Mom.

RUTH: Don't say that.

THOMAS: You said I could… I could think of you as my—

RUTH: I didn't say you could *call* me / your mother…

THOMAS: It's only how I think of it… You had a son, / you told me.

RUTH: Well I don't have a son anymore.

(RUTH swings.)

THOMAS: Maybe he came back.

RUTH: Like a ghost, to say goodbye.

THOMAS: No, like me. To be your son again. I won't go, I promise. Couldn't we pretend I was him?

RUTH: You're nothing like him. *(Swinging.)* I'm alone now. Rid of your house, Arthur. Rid of you for good, talkin' to me the rotten miserable way you do. Eh, Arthur? What do you say to that?! Arthur? Arthur?! Arthur you dirty rotten scumbag! *(Swinging, she listens: silence.)*

THOMAS: You're like my mom, I'm sure. Just like her.

RUTH: My good lord…he's gone. *(Swinging high and jubilant, smiling skyward.)* Yes! I can't hear him! I'm rid of you, Husband! I'm clear! Yes!

THOMAS: *(In awe.)* You're crazy.

RUTH: I'm free! Thank you Jehovah and Elohim! Thank you Odin! Thank you Brahma, Vishnu and Shiva! You wives Juno, Rhea, Persephone, Frigg! Thank you Moloch! Isis, Osiris, Ra! Alpha and O—

(RUTH chokes silently on her candy with shocking, momentarily chilling verisimilitude. Not funny. THOMAS watches, stunned.)

THOMAS: What. What are you doing. Ruth? RUTH! Jeeze, are you…I don't know what to do so you just stop it right now. Come on! *(She looks, grasping at him.)* Help! Somebody please help! Ruth? Are you…are you dying, Mom?

(He gets on top of her.)

Come on, please, please come back. NO! NO! NO!

(He looks hard into her exploding, desperate face. She is sure to die.)

NO!

(He slams her chest, hard. RUTH turns to her side, weakly pushing THOMAS off her. Her eyes are wide and terrified, humbled. She has seen the other side.)

I saved you… Did you see that? *(Ebullient tears.)* I saved your life.

(He fusses with her clothing, straightening her out: clumsy, careful gestures of care. RUTH lies in shock, close against the earth, as if afraid to let her face and the length of her body leave it.)

I love you, Mom. You're mine.

(THOMAS gathers the crumpled newspapers, garbage, Ruth's nearby bags, LONNIE's case, stuffing it all around them, like a nest. RUTH sits herself up and reaches inside her coat. Her hand emerges cradling the remains of an egg.)

RUTH: My duck. My duckling. *(She breaks.)* My duckling…

THOMAS: *(Holding RUTH.)* It's okay, it was just an egg…

RUTH: He's lost…

THOMAS: No, Mom, I'm here.

RUTH: Oh my dear, my dear darling boy.

(Dawn comes. A spectacular sunrise. THOMAS looks about them. He opens LONNIE's case and gazes into it.)

THOMAS: Oh mercy. Mom, look at all the things.

(The End.)

Changing the Geography of *Grace*

The following changes to the script may be made in order to change the setting of *Grace* to fit another city.

p. 15: "Toronto and Chicago" may be changed to other appropriate cities.

p. 16: Depending on the size of the city and the bus they go on, the line:

> HUGH: I've got one of these new condos up here. Nice place: seventeenth floor, good neighbours.

may be changed to a lower floor, or to read:

> HUGH: I've got one of these new strata homes up here. They renovated this big old house into pieces. Nice place: top floor, good neighbours.

p. 30: Change "Reno's" to the name of an appropriate café.

p. 36: Depending on the geography of the city, the hill park may arrive before the cemetery, in which case the line:

> PAULA: Don't know, past here. I got off first.

may be changed to:

> PAULA: Don't know, near the cemetery.

Since Paula would then see Jared get off the bus.

p. 55: Change "12 - 4571 Fraser Street" to an appropriate address.

p. 56: Change "Reno's" as above.

p. 66: Change "Little Mountain" to the name of an appropriate park with a view (preferably different from the park in the second half).